# You're on the Trail!

## CONTENTS

NATIONAL GEOGRAPHIC    Hampton-Brown

School Publishing

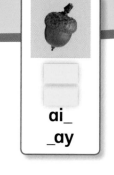

# Words with <u>ai</u>, <u>ay</u>

Look at each picture. Read the words.

ai_
_ay

**Example:**

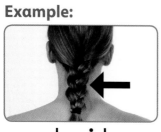

br<u>ai</u>d

ch<u>ai</u>n

p<u>ai</u>nt

cl<u>ay</u>

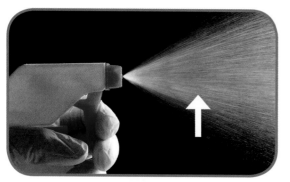

spr<u>ay</u>

tr<u>ay</u>

# Key Words

Look at the pictures.
Read the sentences.

High Frequency
**Words**

| funny |
| hurt |
| light |
| mean |
| sea |
| sound |

prints

## Prints in the Sand

1. I like the **sea**.
2. I like the **sound** of the waves.
3. But the **light** can **hurt** my eyes!
4. Do you see the **funny** prints in the sand?
5. What do they **mean**?

What animal made the prints?

**Phonics Games**
NGReach.com

3

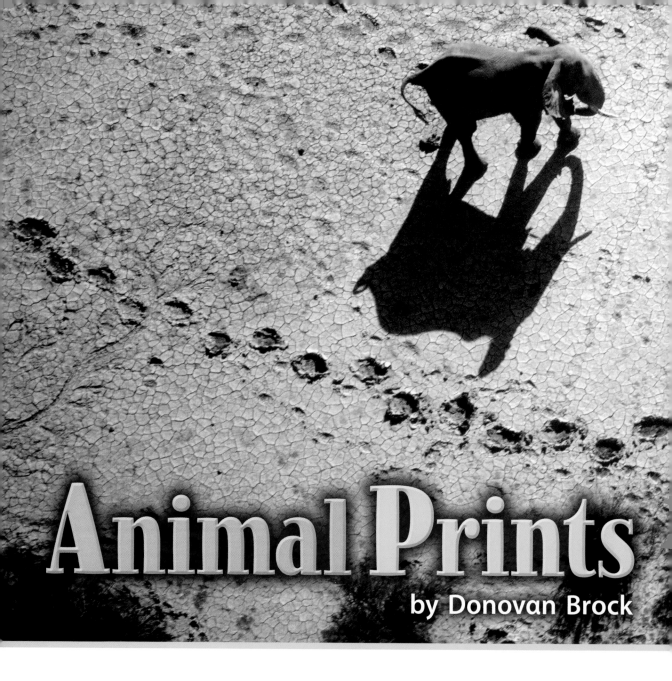

# Animal Prints

by Donovan Brock

Find a trail. Look at it up close.

Do you see animal prints?

sand

mud

clay

Animals walk, run, and jump. They can make prints when they move. You can see their prints in sand, mud, and clay.

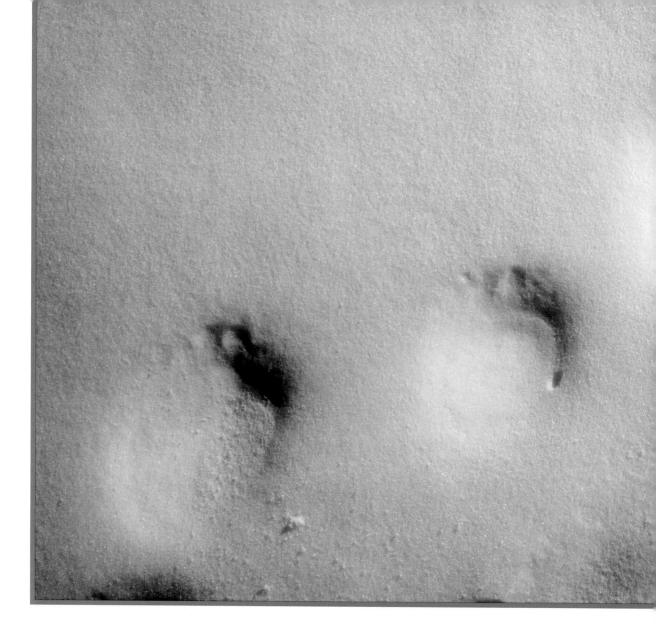

Some prints are faint. You may need training to track them.

tracker

A tracker looks for prints. The size and shape of a print can mean a lot to a trained tracker.

Prints can tell which way an animal moved on its trail. Which way are the feet going?

Not all prints are made by an animal
with feet. Which prints are made by a
snake? Which is a snail's slimy trail?

daylight

dark

You can see animal prints best in the day, when it is light. But many animals move more in the dark.

bat

frog

fox

You can use your ears to track animals in the dark. What animal sounds are around you?

skunk

You can use your nose, too. But watch out! It is not funny when a skunk sprays. You may not want to track a skunk at all! ❖

# Words with <u>ai</u>, <u>ay</u>

Read these words.

| | | | | |
|---|---|---|---|---|
| brain | clay | pail | swing | way |
| bush | grass | sand | train | |

Find the words with **ai** and **ay**. Use letters to build them.

**Talk Together**

Choose words from the box above to tell your partner about the trail through the yard.

The trail goes past a <u>train</u> and through <u>clay</u>.

13

# Contractions

Look at the picutres. See how contractions are made. Read the words.

I am → I ′m → I'm

I'm Ali.

she will → she ′ll → she'll

She'll be home soon.

they are → they ′re → they're

They're having fun.

High Frequency
**Words**

| funny |
| hurt |
| light |
| mean |
| sea |
| sound |

# Key Words

Look at the picture.
Read the sentences.

**A Funny Fish**

1. This **funny** flat fish lives in the **sea**.
2. There is not much **light** or **sound** where it swims.
3. It is a harmless fish. This **means** it won't **hurt** you.

What does *harmless* mean?

**GO! Phonics Games**
NGReach.com

15

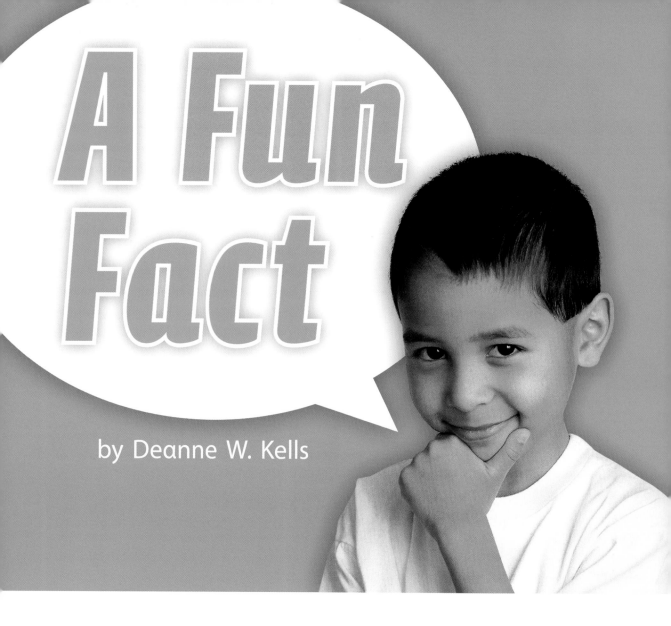

# A Fun Fact

by Deanne W. Kells

I've got a fun fact. Some animals have names that have almost the same sounds. Yet the two animals are not the same at all!

I'll show you what I mean. We'll start with the sole and the mole.

sole

mole

A sole is a flat fish. It swims under water in the sea.

A mole lives under the ground.

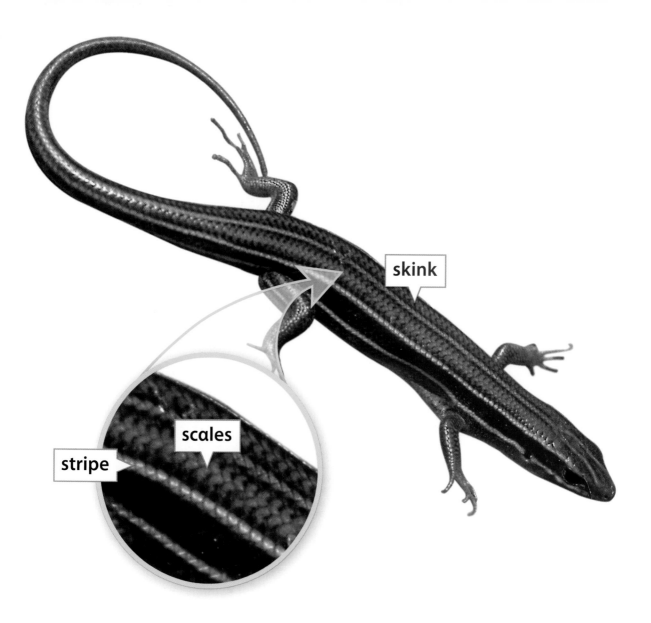

skink

scales

stripe

Look at the skink and the skunk.
They're both striped. But the skink has
scales, and the skunk has hair.

tail

hair

skunk

If you grab the skink's tail, it'll snap off! This will not hurt the skink.

If the skunk lifts its tail, run! It is not funny to get hit with skunk spray.

cat

Look at the cat and the bat. They do
not need a lot of light to see well.

bat

The cat will run to catch mice. But the bat can fly! It'll snap up bugs.

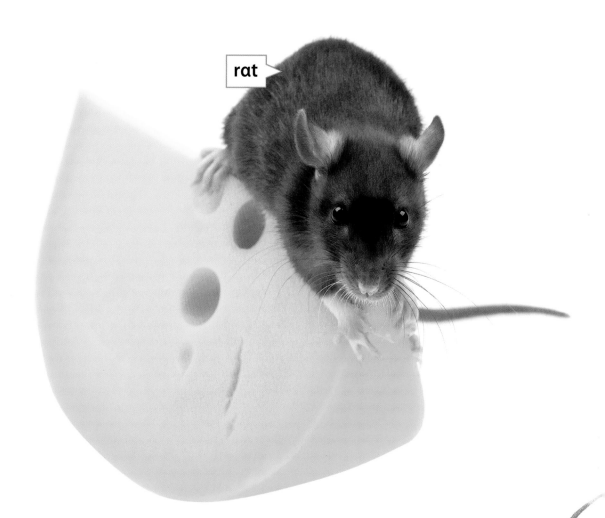

Look at the rat and the ram. A rat is quite small. A rat can bite. So do not get close to a rat.

A ram is quite big. Look at his horns. He'll use them to keep other male rams far from him. He will not hurt you.

Here are some others. I'm going to
give you hints. What's the missing name? ❖

**hog** and ___ ___ ___

**ox** and ___ ___ ___

# Contractions

Read these words.

| | | | |
|---|---|---|---|
| he'll | they'll | drinks | you've |
| she'll | milk | cake | fish |

Find the contractions.
Use letters to build them.

**Talk Together**

Use the pictures
and words from
the box above to
tell your partner
about the cats.

They'll get drinks.

# Animal Train

The circus animals are vain. They like to brag!
Take turns reading their words with a partner.
Match them to the animals.

 My pretty eyes are the color of the
sea. Too much light can hurt them.

 You'll like the paint on my nails.
They match my pink hat!

**3** My long gray nose is quite nice. You'll think it is funny when I grab things with it.

 **4** I'm such a nice shade of gray! I have a fine braid in my mane.

**Acknowledgments**

Grateful acknowledgment is given to the authors, artists, photographers, museums, publishers, and agents for permission to reprint copyrighted material. Every effort has been made to secure the appropriate permission. If any omissions have been made or if corrections are required, please contact the Publisher.

**Photographic Credits**

**CVR** (Cover) Britta Kasholm-Tengve/iStockphoto. **2** (bl) Christine Glade/iStockphoto. (br) Kelly Cline/iStockphoto. (cl) PhotoDisc/Getty Images. (cr) Diane White Rosier/iStockphoto. (tl) Stefan Redel/Shutterstock. (tr) Image Club. **3** (b) Liz Garza Williams/Hampton-Brown/ National Geographic School Publishing. (l) Sarun Laowong/iStockphoto. (r) Doris McKenzie/ iStockphoto. **4-5** (bg) Carlo Mari/Tips Italia/Photolibrary. **5** (c) Eric and David Hosking/Corbis. (l) Frans Lanting/National Geographic Image Collection. (r) Momatiuk - Eastcott/Corbis. **6-7** (bg) altrendo images/Getty Images. **7** Michael Nichols/National Geographic Image Collection. **8** Emily Veinglory/Shutterstock. **9** (l) Bruce Dale/National Geographic Image Collection. (r) Renee Morris/Alamy Images. **10** (l) Johannes Ehrhardt/National Geographic Image Collection. (r) Gunhild Andersen/National Geographic Image Collection. **11** (b) Eric Isselée/iStockphoto. (c) Creatas/Jupiterimages. (t) Cybermedia/PhotoDisc/Getty Images. **12** Creatas/Jupiterimages/Alamy Images. **13** (l) Liz Garza Williams/Hampton-Brown/National Geographic School Publishing. **14** (b) Polka Dot Images/Jupiterimages. (c) Jamie Kripke/Corbis. (t) BananaStock/Jupiterimages. **15** (b) Liz Garza Williams/Hampton-Brown/National Geographic School Publishing. (t) Nature Picture Library/Alamy Images. **16** Digital Vision/Getty Images. **17** (b) Tramper/Shutterstock. (t) Comstock Images/Getty Images. **18** (l) Corel. (r) Corel. **19** Geoff Kuchera/iStockphoto. **20** (b) G.K. & Vikki Hart/Photodisc/Getty Images. (t) John Foxx Images/Imagestate. **21** (b) G.K. & Vikki Hart/Photodisc/Getty Images. (c) Michael Durham/ Minden Pictures. (l) Artville. (r) Artville. **22** (b) PhotoDisc/Getty Images. (t) Ragnarocks/ iStockphoto. **23** Chris Johns/National Geographic Image Collection. **24** (bl) Hemera Technologies/Getty Images/Jupiterimages. (br) PhotoDisc/Getty Images. (tl) PhotoDisc/Getty Images. (tr) Artville. **25** (l) Liz Garza Williams/Hampton-Brown/National Geographic School Publishing.

**Illustrator Credits**

**13** Erika LeBarre. **14** Peter Grosshauser. **25-27** Erika LeBarre

**The National Geographic Society**

John M. Fahey, Jr., President & Chief Executive Officer
Gilbert M. Grosvenor, Chairman of the Board

National Geographic School Publishing
Hampton-Brown
www.NGSP.com

Printed in the USA.
RR Donnelley, Jefferson City, MO

ISBN: 978-0-7362-8040-2

12 13 14 15 16 17 18 19
10 9 8 7 6 5 4

## New High Frequency Words

funny
hurt
light
mean
sea
sound

## Target Sound/Spellings

| Vowel Digraphs ai, ay | Contractions |
|---|---|
| **Selection:** **Animal Prints** | **Selection:** **A Fun Fact** |
| clay | he'll |
| day | I'll |
| faint | I'm |
| may | it'll |
| snail | I've |
| sprays | they're |
| trail(s) | |
| train(ed) | |
| training | |
| way | |